G000111329

The
Importance
of
Book Cover
Design
and
Formatting

The
Importance
of
Book Cover
Design
and
Formatting

For Self-Published Authors

JD Smith

The Importance of Book Cover Design and Formatting © 2016 JD Smith

The moral rights of the author have been asserted.

All rights reserved. No part of this publication may be reproduced, distributed, or transmitted in any form or by any means, including photocopying, recording, or other electronic or mechanical methods, without the prior written permission of the publisher, except in the case of brief quotations embodied in critical reviews and certain other non-commercial uses permitted by copyright law. For permission requests, write to the publisher, addressed "Attention: Permissions Coordinator," at the email address below.

Book covers used as examples are either designed by JD Smith or are used under UK Intellectual Property Guidance, Exceptions to Copyright: "Criticism, review and reporting current events. Fair dealing for criticism, review or quotation is allowed for any type of copyright work."

Cover design and formatting www.jdsmith-design.com

Published by Quinn Publications

All enquiries to info@jdsmith-design.co.uk

First published 2016

ISBN: 978-0-9576164-9-3

This book is dedicated to my clients,
who have allowed me to do a job I love,
and create beautiful books.

Contents

Introduction

I've been in the book design industry for some years now, and before that I worked for a branding agency. I have hundreds of books on my shelves I've not had the chance to read, because I have an addiction to buying beautiful books with stunning covers. I spend a lot of time scrolling through book covers and as much as I do that as part of my job, I love every minute surrounded by aesthetically pleasing and technically well-designed books.

For me book covers are about selling books. They are about fitting the genre and appealing to the right market. I'm a sentimentalist but also a realist. Most authors and publishers put books out into the world to either be found, or to be found and make money. If we publish books just to gather dust on one of Amazon's virtual shelves, we might as well have left them on our hard drives. And from a personal perspective, I feel we writers owe it to our books to make them the best they can possibly be.

Over the years I have been asked a lot of questions, both as a fellow indie author and as a book designer, about the world of publishing. Things change, and with more and more authors receiving their rights back for previously traditionally published books, or wanting to publish backlists for which they never signed away ebook rights, as well as new authors who have either been unsuccessful in securing a deal with a publisher or have chosen to indie publish because it suits them, there are a lot of authors out there unsure of how to approach the publishing process.

This book isn't a how to create your own book cover guide (although I will include some links if you do choose to DIY), but aims to provide you with insight into how important book cover design and good formatting is and why, including examples of what makes a good book cover and interior and what doesn't. I will also explain the common mistakes made when doing it yourself, as well as advise on looking for and working with a book designer, link to the best stock image sites, link to printers for marketing materials, talk about budgeting, include case studies and a useful glossary of design terms.

I hope this book gives you an insight into the world of book design. I want to arm you with the knowledge you need to be able to choose and work with a designer, to make informed decisions about your book cover design, and to have the best chance of publishing success.

Remember, one of the best things about being an independent author is that you can not only have a professional cover that sells, you can also have one you love.

Enjoy!

Jane (JD Smith)

Chapter 1
The Importance of Cover Design

There's a constant debate about the relevance and importance of cover design, whether you're a self-published author, part of a collective group of authors, an independent press, or even a large publishing house. If you are publishing your book to give away as Christmas presents, or you only expect a few members of your family to buy them, then the cover is as important as you consider it to be. But if you are a professional writer and you intend to earn a living or be taken seriously in the literary world, then the book cover is as important as the copy editing, the proofreading, the story and the characters. It is a part of your marketing ... and it's there to attract the right kind of readers.

I've heard of professionally designed covers being criticized because there is free software available with which an author can create their own covers. This is true, there are lots of tools out there: Paint, CorelDRAW, Gimp ... (if you haven't heard of the latter, it's an image manipulation tool downloadable from the web). The fact is, these tools aren't professional tools, and even if they were they are only as good as the people using them. Don't use expensive software for the sake of it. However, most of the time, it is necessary to achieve professional results.

Cover design is one area where independent presses continually fall down as they try to put books to market as cheaply as possible. It's a complaint many authors make when they've decided to accept a contract with a small publisher; not only did they have little or no say in the cover design, but the designs they were presented with and expected to agree on were nothing short of dire.

The fact is that book covers spurred the greatest cliché in history – never judge a book by its cover – but no matter how much we want to believe people won't, they do. People, food, places, but most of all, books.

Why is a book cover important?

This always seems so obvious to me but for others it is less so. So here goes, I'm going to explain exactly why book covers are important.

A book cover attracts the reader and encourages them to pick up your book

Bookshops display books with their covers facing the reader. It's the first thing a reader sees and the reason a customer picks up the book, particularly in a supermarket setting where most if not all books are front facing. Even the author can be recognised not only by the letters spelling their name, but by the font, the style of cover, composition, the look of a series.

Only when a reader has picked up the book do they actually read anything, and that includes the back cover blurb that you will have spent hours and hours honing. If the blurb was worth all that effort, then the cover is equally if not more deserving.

The reasons why a person will pick up your book are many and varied.

- They might pick it up because they recognise your brand or series styling.

- Because the cover design gives a good sense of the genre and the reader is looking for something in that genre.

- It's simply eye-catching.

- It reminds them of another author they really like.

- The title really struck them.

- They have to have the book because they fell in love with the cover (this is me).

Some people deem ebook covers to be less important than paperback covers because they aren't a physical object. This makes me want to talk about cluttering the market with badly edited, written, proofed and formatted books, because it saturates the market with crap and gives indie authors a bad name, but we'll leave that for a blog post. However, the rules that apply to bookshops are true of online retailers. You can be searching Amazon or the iBookstore or any other ebook retailer, or you can open an email newsletter, and the first thing you will be presented with is a cover, or a series of covers, and instead of picking up the book to read the blurb you click on a cover instead.

Even when, on Amazon and other online retailers, books are displayed as a list, the main thing your eye is drawn to is the cover, because the list of titles and authors are all presented in the same font, size, and colour.

The same applies to advertising. A customer's eye is drawn by the cover, the design of the advert, and the wording used to grab attention.

Even on recommendation, a reader might not pick up a book or read the blurb because the cover is so off-putting for one reason or another.

Why?

Because a book's cover is its face. It generates expectation. If a reader sees an amateur cover, they will expect the novel itself to be amateur. If it looks cheaply produced, then they will expect the inside quality to be equally cheap – little or no editing, proofreading, or containing bad prose.

And if a reader sees a cover and has that expectation, why should they buy it? Convince me? Because honestly it has been properly edited and proofread? I'm not buying that. My assessment has been made and I'm not picking it up.

In fairness, a reader probably hasn't gone through the thought process far enough to know they've made an assumption on the quality of the interior. They simply glanced at the cover then moved on.

And it's not just about someone buying a book, it's about them investing their time reading it. A book takes a good number of hours to read. I make a decision to read a book less lightly than choosing a film or a TV programme to watch. My time is precious. And the more dubious the quality of material that is out there, the more discerning readers will become.

But I'll get reviews and their recommendation will pave the way to thousands of sales, I hear you say. WRONG. I'm the editor of the readers' blog, www.bookmuse.co.uk, and part of our submissions process is vetting for bad covers. It is THE first hurdle. If the cover isn't good, I don't even send the book on to the review team. If the cover isn't up to scratch, we won't be reviewing your book, and the same goes for a lot of review sites, even small ones. Why? Because it's the reputation of my review site at stake. I don't want readers clicking through to see an awful cover and leaving as quickly as they arrived. I want them to have faith in our recommendations as an author should want a reader to have faith in their book.

Can I have a cover as good as a traditionally published book?

Big publishers spend thousands on a cover to ensure it's right, commissioning illustration and photography. It's normal for publishers such as Hodder & Stoughton to have 50+ covers designed for a single book so they get it 'just right'. It's the reason publishers design different book covers for different countries, markets and so on. They have the budget; they also have a lot of decision makers, so the process inevitably takes longer and costs more.

That doesn't mean to say self-published authors and collectives etc. can't have covers that are equally as professional as those produced by major publishers for a fraction of the cost.

A close working relationship between author and designer can produce some intimate and spectacular results. The wrong designer and you can end up with something that looks like it's been produced by someone who should not have been allowed to use Photoshop, never mind call themselves a designer. Just because someone calls themselves a designer doesn't mean they're good at it. Likewise, a person doesn't need a degree in graphics to be able to design marketable covers.

Here's a test. Can you tell which covers are designed by a traditional publishing house and which have been commissioned by indie authors?

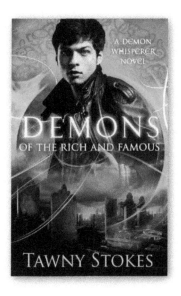

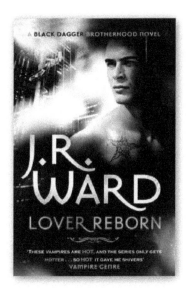

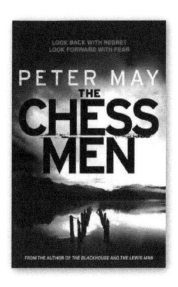

Not easy, is it? Tawny Stokes and Eliza Green are the indie authors here.

Of course it's easy to get it wrong, too…

 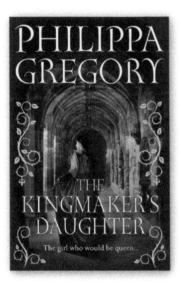

I'm assuming you've guessed correctly that the cover on the left isn't professionally designed. Where do I start? Well, the book's title isn't centred, the font is cheap looking, the title could have been moved down so it didn't clash with the girl's hand, the author name is stretched, and difficult to read because it's grey on grey, and the image looks like it's been stripped off a bridal magazine.

So where do I start here? Okay, *On Dublin Street* uses beautiful typography for the title, with the subtle and sophisticated '*On*', the muted tones create a lovely mood, the strapline is short and snappy, the author's name is in a colour which really reflects the rest of the cover. It's not huge, but it's still legible because of the spacing and being a light colour on a dark background. As for the other cover, I actually can't make out the title because of the font, the gradient colours used, and the image is little better. I think it's meant to be steamy, but it's just blurry.

If you fancy critiquing a few covers yourself, www.lousybookcovers.com has a great supply.

A different cover for ebook and paperback?

I am asked this question a lot. Physically, the difference between an ebook cover and a paperback cover is that an ebook cover is just the front cover of the book, with no spine or back cover. It is a JPEG that is submitted to Amazon Kindle or Smashwords etc. when you upload your ebook, and will then be displayed on sales websites and on reading devices. Whereas a paperback is the front, spine and back cover of a physical book, sized in either inches or mm to accommodate your chosen finish size and page count.

There is no reason why the front cover of both the ebook and the paperback can't be the same. Ebooks are clearly labelled as ebooks on sites such as Amazon, so there is no need to add any additional wording to your cover such as 'Kindle Edition'.

In the past I've heard predictions that ebook covers would become less like covers and more like icons because of their display size on online shops, but that isn't the case, and major publishers are still putting out covers which are the same as the paperback or hardback editions. Occasionally there's a slight differential, other times they do change completely, although I tend to think this has more to do with the publisher feeling that the original cover didn't work as well as they'd thought, or that they are targeting the ebook version to a different market.

For example, *Gone Girl*, published by Weidenfeld & Nicolson, Orion, has same cover for ebook, paperback and audio (only square to fit with audiobook standards). It was only the hard-cover that was different.

I would rarely recommend that a self-published author go to the expense of having separate designs done for ebook and paperback unless they had a very good marketing reason behind their decision.

Chapter 2

The Fundamentals
of Cover Design

Good cover design doesn't just refer to the amount of time or money spent on it. A cover I've designed isn't better because I've spent twice as many hours on it as another book, or twice as many images. A cover can be simple and equally as effective. It can be the first design I've done for a specific book rather than the third. It's all about hitting the right balance between images, text, colour and so on. There are many elements within a cover that make it work.

Let's use Linzé Brandon's book, *Keeper of the Dragon Sword*, as an example.

- Good imagery
- Good colour choice
- Good font choice

Good Imagery:

Imagery should be suitable to the period in which the book is set. Here, in a dark-ages style fantasy epic, the images chosen are relevant – the hair on the man isn't a modern cut, neither character wears modern clothes, the sword is ancient, and the woman isn't wearing make-up or appears as if posing for Vogue.

The other important key here is that the overall cover is made up of multiple images. A common mistake is to blend images into one another, but not correct the colours in the images so they match. Here a yellow filter has been placed on the image of the woman so she fits with the overall yellow-ish tint of the rest of the cover.

In addition, the background behind the text is darker so that the text is visible and doesn't blur into the background, making it hard to read.

Good Colour Choice:

It's vital to use colours which stand out; white and black here. When using a colour, it should be a hue picked out of the imagery used, or a direct complement. It shouldn't just be a random colour, which clashes with everything else.

Good Contrast:

Contrast will make a cover really stand out. Here we've got a stark contrast between the male figure and the background behind him, together with the paleness of her face, which makes the cover jump. This can be achieved in other ways, such as using strong colours, light on dark and dark on light.

Good Font Choice:

The font needs to be something in keeping with the style of the book. If you look at covers in your genre, you'll notice a trend: Chick-Lit using curly, girly fonts; Historical Romance script fonts; Action solid, impact style typefaces; Literary Fiction often uses classic serifs or light sans-serifs and so on. It's not strict, but chosen right the font will say as much about the contents of the book as the image. Get it wrong and it'll either look bad or will appeal to the wrong audience.

Good Typography:

The composition of the title and author name are really important in creating a professional feel. Here you'll notice that the title is stacked. Note that the left hand edge of the 'K' of 'Keeper' is aligned with the left hand edge of the 'R' of 'Dragon' and so on, whilst at the same time 'Of The' is right aligned with the last letter of 'Dragon'. It fits in a grid which, when locked tightly together, is therefore attractive to the eye.

Good Composition:

Composition is very much a grid. Look at your subject and set up your shot to a grid. Below you'll notice that the title takes up approximately a third of the lower half of the page, whilst the characters two thirds. Whereas the horizontal composition is constructed of the man on one half and the woman on the other half, with the sword running through the middle. That's a little general as it doesn't always work quite like that, but there's always a balance to be reached.

- Good typography

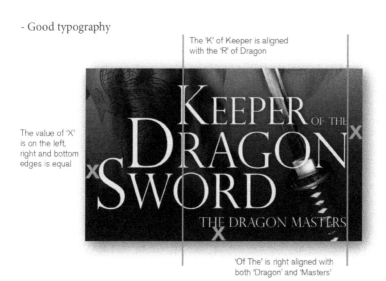

The 'K' of Keeper is aligned with the 'R' of Dragon

The value of 'X' is on the left, right and bottom edges is equal

'Of The' is right aligned with both 'Dragon' and 'Masters'

Another trick is to line the text up so that it's of equal distance from, say, the top edge of the page to the right and left hand sides. If it's not going to be equal, it needs to be deliberately unequal, otherwise it just looks poorly positioned. These are just examples, not global rules, of subtle things designers do subconsciously to make sure the cover is balanced.

These are all things that designers are trained to do, or they've got an eye for, or they have learned over time. But good design isn't just about these elements, and making good or bad choices with regards to what a good font or a bad font is.

It's also about **wrong** choices.

Chapter 3
Reaching YOUR Readers

When you put your book out in the marketplace, your cover works as an advert in itself. You are using it to advertise your novel, your product. Think how irritating it is when you see an advert on television for something and when you buy it and take it home, you discover it isn't what you thought it was. The same applies to books.

If a reader purchases a book they think is Crime Fiction, because the cover has all the tell-tale signs of Crime Fiction, then they may like the Romantic Fiction you have graced the pages with, but the likelihood is they will be sorely disappointed. The unwritten contract you have with your reader has been broken because you have given them a cover which does not resemble what is inside.

Of course it's unlikely you will make the mistake of pushing crime fiction onto a romance reader. It's more likely that the cover won't shriek crime, so it will be passed over. That said, I have personally bought books thinking they were historical fiction only to find they were a modern-day mystery. I also bought a copy of *The Duchess* with Keira Knightley on the front, thinking it was a novel based on the film. Wrong. It was a biography. You have no idea how hugely disappointed I was. It's one of the few books I've given away.

It's like having a can labelled Baked Beans, only to discover when you open the tin that it contains peas …

You can see from the images that there is a distinct range of covers which really shout what they're about. George R. R. Martin has a typical fantasy feel, with a sword that is more elven then Saxon. *Eighty Days of Blue* copies the *Fifty Shades* look with its heavy black cover (note that the title is quite small – it doesn't matter, because the title isn't selling that book, *Fifty Shades* is selling it). *Thursday in the Park* has a really fun, rom-com feel. You know you'll feel good at the end. Bernard Cornwell, typical historical novel. He's the male version of Philippa Gregory with a blood-splattered breastplate in replace of a luxurious Tudor frock. *Enduring Love* shrieks literary fiction with a hot air balloon, man dangling from a rope and muted colours. Iain M. Banks has a token planet at the bottom of the cover despite the tell-tale "M." inserted into his name denoting it's one of his sci-fi novels. Nothing says apocalyptic zombie novel quite like a barren countryside with a silhouette figure running away like *The Walking Dead* does. And lastly Ann Cleeves, who's echoing a popular trend for bleak yet strong landscapes for crime fiction.

All of the authors I featured are big names (bar the exception Vina Jackson, who is trading on *Fifty Shades* fame and who I admit I have never heard of), proving that even authors who are well known have book covers that fit with their genre rather than obscure covers that don't give any clue as to the type of book they are.

One client came to me with a book for which she had just gained the rights back. Originally published by one of the Big 4, the book was a *contemporary* literary fiction novel. The publisher, for a reason known only to them and their marketing team, put a medieval tapestry on the cover. It looked like a Philippa Gregory style book, something an historian turned novelist had written. They got it wrong and they knew they had. They later reprinted the title with a more fitting set of obscure trees, reflecting both the genre and the book's theme.

What about cover cliché?

Articles on cover clichés with writers poking fun of book covers with similar covers or pointing out patterns or trends can be a fun read, but they're missing the point.

Covers which are branded similarly to other books that are already selling well will also sell well. Why? It's a marker, a sign that says if you like that book you'll like this book. Bucking the trend is risky. You risk losing the readers of the authors whose audience you're marketing to.

This is the main reason I ask authors to research and send me covers in their genre that they like. I don't research the covers myself for two reasons. Firstly, I'm not as well read in other people's genres as they are, so they know specifically which writers are closest to their writing. And secondly, I want them to choose covers they like, because I want to create covers that sell, but I don't want clients to hate the end result.

Book covers which relate the essence of a book are but don't convey the genre or theme can be beautiful. Indeed, they can be anything but cliché, and they appeal visually. Will they make people buy your book? Possibly, but probably not. Going for something out of the ordinary and pushing the boundaries of graphic design can give you a unique book cover, but unless you're a major publishing house backing it with a weighty marketing budget, or a huge name author (think J.K. Rowling's *Casual Vacancy*), then you aren't going to sell books and your aim will be way off your target audience.

Trying to tell your story on the cover

Authors often make the mistake of trying to cram their full-length novel onto the cover, featuring several characters, four different scenes and three different murder weapons. The cover isn't the place to tell your story, that's why you wrote the book!

Instead, focus on genre-specific, attractive, eye-catching imagery. It has to *relate* to your story and genre, but it doesn't need to *tell* the story.

When it comes to nonfiction, again it depends on where the book is marketed. If we use a How-To book as an example, the title and sub-title tend to be the most important aspect, depending on what the book is about. That's what will sell. People who are looking to make a million want the book to say, How to Make a Million. And the title should convey that. Here you want supportive imagery. Something which encompasses the book's message. The readers here are hungry for information and they want to be told the book will give them that.

Getting specific about images

Time and time again I have clients who get caught up with the images on the cover needing to exactly match the very specific description they have in chapter 28 of their novel. That's okay if you're commissioning an illustration or photography, but much less easy when working with stock images.

Now I personally can manipulate images pretty well. I can change eye colour and hair colour and erase the odd tattoo and Photoshop in a different background. I can apply filters to change the over colour in an image from, say, warm to cool and so on. Designers can do a lot. But what they can't do is take a shot of a woman facing the camera and turn her around so she's facing away. It doesn't work like that.

And despite there being thousands upon thousands of stock images available, when you're looking for very specific items, then the choice starts to become very limited.

It's best to be open to what's available and not sacrifice a good cover design for a poor photograph that has just the right angle of a centaur's rear.

Straplines, quotes and thumbnails

But they won't be seen in thumbnail, I hear people chorus. No, probably not. So why have them? 'It needs to work in thumbnail' is one of the most overused phrases in publishing these days. It's also one of the least understood.

Not everything on the cover has to be visible when your book is thumbnail size. And what is thumbnail exactly? Because I don't have small thumbnails, and looking on my Android phone at the list of books that come up when you search, the covers are at least a third larger than my thumbnail. So I'm starting a petition: I think we need to stop using the phrase thumbnail and default to postage stamp size instead.

Anyway, back to what needs to be visible. This actually depends on your genre and market. Not all markets lean toward the title and author name as being important, for example. You generally need to be able to make out something, whether that's the image, the title or the author. You'll rarely be able to make them all out, and you definitely won't be able to make out a strapline or quote.

So what's the point of having one? Well for starters, it will be visible if not legible, so a reader will know it's there. Lots of traditional books have one or the other or both, and so your book can appear more professional. It also gives a subtle indicator that you've been endorsed by a big name author, or that the strapline might state that you are a NY Times Bestseller.

Award badges sell books

It's widely known that receiving a book award (e.g. Sci-Fi book of the year 2032) will appeal to readers and sell more books. And that's true. And the award people will send you a badge that you can plaster all over your website, social media and book cover. Great! You can advertise the fact that you have an award and more people will pick up your book.

But be careful. It's really nice to be able to put an award badge on your cover, but not to the detriment of your book cover. Some award badges are really nice and tasteful and make your book look more prestigious, and others are tacky and badly designed and will do your book no favours. It's like I said earlier about people believing in the quality of your book because of the quality of the cover. They won't believe an award badge is worth anything if it looks like a five-year-old made it on their bounce-proof tablet.

To Summarise:

- Make sure your cover appeals to YOUR genre and target audience

- Don't worry about cover cliché

- Try not to cram too much on the cover

- Don't expect everything to show up at postage stamp size

- Be careful which award badges you add to your cover.

Chapter 4
Stock Images vs. Commissioned

Stock images

Stock images are images that have been taken for people to use or buy permission to use for a variety of purposes.

Most stock image libraries are royalty-free. This means you pay a fee for permission to use an image within the terms laid out by the stock image library. So for example, Shutterstock. com has a variety of packages. You can purchase 5 image credits for around £32, or you can pay a monthly fee and download as many images as you like per day, and can be physically reproduced 500,000 times – so you could print 500,000 books with the image on. The licensing agreement isn't exactly as to the point as that, but you get the idea. You would need to check licenses for individual sites for specific details of their license agreements and how many times you can use an image within their agreement.

Some images can only be used for editorial and not commercial use. Lots of images come with the option of buying an extended license. This usually gives unlimited reproductions, and use on things like merchandise and templates—for example, if you were to sell posters with an image printed on, so basically the product is the image, rather than a book where people are buying the book for its contents.

There are also plenty of sites offering **free images** (often for a mention of the photographer on the copyright page). These are okay but of course you get what you pay for, and mostly they aren't great images.

There are also sites which offer **rights-managed** images. These are usually more expensive and are priced on application depending on how much you want to use them, for what time period, and in which regions. For example, Archangel images sent me this rough price guide:

Ebook only, UK or single territory: £200 to £350

Print & ebook rights, UK Commonwealth: £400 to £600

Print & ebook rights, World English Language: £850 or more

And lastly there are sites which occasionally offer **exclusive licenses** for a larger fee than a non-exclusive license. This means they will sell the image to you and only you, so no one else can use that exact image on their book cover. The problem here is that the photoshoot has many images all taken of the same model, in the same outfit, just in a very marginally different pose, so it's really not worth buying an exclusive license.

Commissioned

And then of course there is the option of **commissioning illustration or photography**, so that your cover is completely unique and you get exactly what you want. This is great for those with a good budget who want something really bespoke. Costs vary depending on illustrator or photograph experience and skill, or just how in demand they are. Bear in mind if you're looking for a specific shot of a man dressed in a knight's costume, for example, you'll need to source a model and a costume, pay for both, and have the model sign a model release.

The terms of which you commission the illustration or photography is between you and them. Most illustrators and photographers will want to retain copyright. Indeed copyright is automatically theirs unless you enter a written agreement to transfer ownership, so don't assume that because you commissioned it you own the final image.

My advice is to always make sure you enter a written agreement and that both parties are happy with the terms before any work is done and any money changes hands. That way there'll be no nasty comeback months down the line.

They're using the same images as me!

If you're using royalty-free, non-exclusive images, that probably will happen. Don't get hung up on it.

As you'll see above, stock images are cheap and easy to access. Rights-managed are more expensive, and therefore less likely to be used by other indie authors, but are still stock images and available for more than one person to use.

Just because the image on your cover is on another author's cover isn't going to make your cover less attractive to your audience, it just means the photographer earns a bit more money for their work. Plus, if your designer is using more than one image on your cover, and potentially manipulating them too, they won't look too similar.

One thing you can do is check the top 100 books in your genre just in case any successful authors are using an image you intend to use. But with so many new images being uploaded to stock libraries every single day, there are literally millions to choose from.

Do stock images make me look amateur?

Not in the slightest, if you pick the right ones. Stock images can be extremely good quality, and you'll find that a lot of big publishing houses use stock images as well. Sometimes higher priced rights-managed images, other times lower cost images.

Then by Julie Myerson and published by Random House uses images from Getty, Corbis, Millennium Images and Alamy.

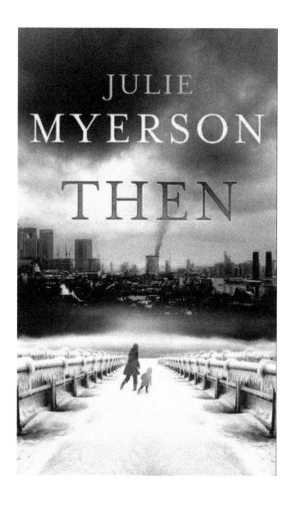

Lady Isobel's Champion by Carol Townend and published by Mills & Boon uses an image available on istockphoto.com for around £20.

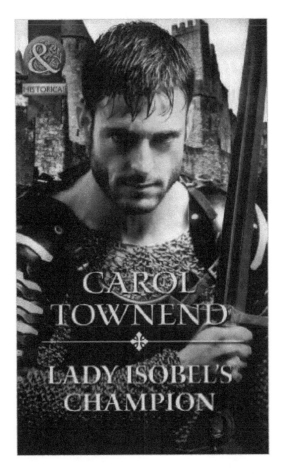

And they are just two I have sat on my bookshelf.

Stock Image Libraries

Here's a list of useful stock image sites:

Wide range of images at reasonable prices

www.shutterstock.com

www.istockphoto.com

www.123rf.com

www.dreamstime.com

Other general image sites

www.thinkstockphotos.co.uk

www.stockfresh.com

www.canstockphoto.com

www.bigstockphoto.com

https://en.fotolia.com/

Free images

www.freerangestock.com

www.freeimages.com

www.totallyfreeimages.com

Romance and historical romance images

www.periodimages.com

www.romancenovelcovers.com

www.hotdamnstock.com

www.razzdazzstock.com

www.novelexpression.com

Rights managed
(generally much more expensive than royalty free)

www.corbisimages.com

www.gettyimages.co.uk

www.alamy.com

www.arcangel.com

www.trevillion.com

www.milim.com

To Summarise:

- It's okay to use stock images

- Don't worry about other people using the same images as you

- If you commission illustration or photography make sure you have a written agreement.

Chapter 5
Finding a Book Cover Designer

Having worked with authors for years, and being an author myself, I know just how personal your book cover is, and just how important it is to find the right cover designer for you.

I would always say go with recommendations from other authors or publishing professionals. If they have worked with someone they are happy with then the likelihood is you will be satisfied with them too.

Ask fellow authors how the process with the designer went, the sort of timescale the project took, the good and bad points. Look extensively at a designer's portfolio. Remember that not all book cover designers are suitable for all genres – some can design across the board, in multiple genres, successfully, but others excel in certain areas. You need to be confident they can do a good job on your book. As in many things in life, cheap is not always best, but expensive is not always necessary.

Questions you need to ask are whether their fee is for ebook cover design or paperback, how many revisions you might expect to receive, how much will they charge for amendments once you've signed off on your cover? Can they provide social media banners and what the cost would be? Can they provide you with layout files and raw images once you're finished? I would always recommend asking for these as it means if you need, for example, your spine width tweaked at a later date and your designer is unavailable, you can pass the files on to someone else and ask them to do it.

It's also worth checking if potential designers offer formatting/typesetting services. It makes a huge visual difference when you have continuity between the interior and cover of a paperback book.

One other, very important point to make is that a graphic designer is not the same thing as an artist or an illustrator. Many times I've seen or heard of people using an illustrator to 'design' a cover, flyer, etc. Illustration is similar to photography. An illustrator will create the imagery, but the layout and composition and typography come under the umbrella of Graphic Design, and an artist, illustrator, or photographer may not necessarily be able to successfully and fully maximise the potential of the imagery they create in realising your cover design.

Usually, and essentially, a graphic designer will work with (a) stock illustration and photography, which is readily available and royalty-free – this is usually the cheaper option, and therefore the most common practice when it comes to self-published authors and small presses. Or (b) your designer will work together either with an illustrator or photographer that you wish to work with, or with one they have sourced and recommend.

When you find a graphic designer you think may be a good fit for your book, be clear with them about what type of cover you want and what your budget is, not least because they can then recommend whether to use affordable imagery or commission photography or illustration.

Lastly, if you've done your homework and engage with a designer who is both experienced and knowledgeable of the publishing industry, then they'll guide you through what they need and what they want from you in order to produce a book cover you like that fits your target market. If they ask the right questions and you provide exactly what they need, you should feel like they've magically read your mind and you'll be really excited by the outcome of the design process …

What if I want to design myself?

Here's a few resources for designing your own cover:

www.canva.com/create/book-covers

www.covercreator.net

www.createspace.com/Special/Help/Tools/
CoverCreatorBooks.jsp

www.diybookcovers.com

To Summarise:

- Ask fellow authors for recommendations

- Check out their portfolios

- Don't expect an amazing design for the price of a coffee, but likewise don't pay over the odds in the hope your cover will be awesome

- Remember an illustrator is not the same as a graphic designer

- Be clear about your budget.

Chapter 6
The Process of Cover Design

What will a designer ask for?

A designer should ask you for the following when working with you:

Blurb/story outline

They'll need a blurb, outline or synopsis to give them an idea of the story. It doesn't have to be agent-worthy, it's just to give them a feel for your book and the characters and locations you feature. Likewise the blurb at this stage doesn't need to be the final blurb for the back cover of a paperback. You can supply that later.

Sample covers

This is the one thing I always ask for, even if a client seems reluctant to supply any. It's such an important part of the process. You'll need to send links to or images of covers that are both in the genre of your book and that you like.

I can't stress enough how key this is to achieving a good end result. People have said to me a few times that there is either 'nothing they like', or that 'there aren't any books out there like mine'. Both of which are rubbish. It's laziness and, as the author, you know your book best. It's important to reflect where it will sit in the marketplace – this is the same information agents ask you when you submit to them. This is the most straightforward, efficient, and ultimately cost-effective way to ensure you get something that both reflects the genre you're writing in and will work in YOUR marketplace.

Elements from the book that you feel could work on the cover

I'm listing this after sample covers because the sample covers can determine the type of thing that will be suitable for your genre. It might be that a text-heavy cover with a background colour or texture would work better than people. Or you realise after looking at other covers that having people on the cover is a definite 'no'. Should the cover be obscure or should it have a location-based image?

If you're talking specifics, such as including a character, then they'll need a rough description, such as hair colour, etc. It's not worth getting too specific, nor expecting too much. A designer will look for images that will work well on your cover and create a really good and saleable design, rather than making sure a model in a stock photo is wearing a specific brand of shoes to fit a very specific scene. Cover design isn't about mimicking a very specific scene in a book, but having a general appeal to your target audience and making them pick up your book.

It doesn't matter whether the covers have the same elements on them that you want on yours, or whether they look different to how you feel you want your cover to look. Your designer should see traits in the covers that work across them all, and also get a good idea of what appeals to you.

Text

Book title, author name, subtitle, strapline, review quotes, back cover blurb. You don't necessarily need to supply all this straight away, but your cover designer will need this information at some point. You'd be amazed how many authors send me their blurb, sample covers and descriptions of elements from their book, but forget to send the title …

A note on your manuscript

Most cover designers won't read your book. They don't need to. Technically speaking it isn't necessary, and the small budgets won't allow for the time it takes. Even in large publishing houses the designer would perhaps read a scene specific to the cover as opposed to a whole book. It's up to the marketing man (be that a marketing person in a big publishing house or yourself as an independent author) to know where the book will sit in the marketplace. If a designer asks for the right information, and you provide it, they will have everything they need to produce a great cover for your market.

The Design Process – project overview

The way each designer works will be slightly different, but here I'll give you an overview on the general process I work through with clients so you have an idea. Jessica had a very specific idea for what she wanted on her cover. Some clients do, most don't. She supplied her blurb together with a photograph of a painting she had done illustrating her main character with half a human face and half a dragon face. She also sent a handful of covers in her target market.

Follow Jamie into her darkest moments. With revenge deftly playing in come to terms with her new enemies. There is only one Aura left for he of her brother, the Australians, and the old, strangely familiar dragon to death over and over again. Along with the dangerous mission before t exactly how she is going to destroy the Auras once they are all placed accept the numerous prophecies starring the yellow-headed dragon. the Foretelling was a mere ploy to convince Jamie to help her.

While Jamie is on her search for the Aura of Life, Samara is preparing for battle; a battle that was foretold would end the war once and for all. But another prophecy is brewing. A prophecy in which Samara will receive the Power of the Auras and end the reign of humans in fire and dust. Will Jamie be able to destroy the Auras in time? Or are all the prophecies about her wrong?

Supply your designer with a rough blurb/outline of your book, any ideas you have, any elements from the book you feel would represent the novel.

"I have a very detailed idea for this cover, and if you'd like I could send you a picture of my sketch. To give you an idea, it involves half of a young woman's face and the other half a yellow dragon's to show that the two are one in the same (it's a contemporary fantasy novel)."

Research books that fit in your genre and that you like.

 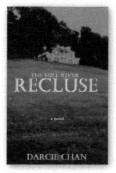 

From there I set about sourcing images which would work on her cover. We needed a model with red hair, almost fantasy looking, with minimal makeup. And we needed a dragon. Here are the images I found and sent to Jessica. They are all stock images ranging from £6 - £25 per image. You'll notice they all have the stock image site's watermarks across them. These are removed on the final hi-resolution images that are used.

Jessica narrowed down the images to a few she felt really worked for her and the descriptions of her character. She chose these six, the landscapes intended for the back cover.

And from there I mocked up rough visuals based on those images. I had to tweak the colours to match and merge the images together, but all that is achievable in Photoshop. She was very specific about what she wanted, and I believed in the concept too, so I only created visuals based on that concept. You'll notice the fonts fit with the genre samples.

Stage 1 - Rough visuals

A  B

Based on Jessica's feedback I then tweaked the visuals further. She was happy with the images on visual A, so I downloaded these and Photoshopped the hi-resolution images, replacing the watermarked ones. This is the point where I really start to tweak and make subtle variations until everyone is happy with the final front cover.

Stage 3 - finalising cover fonts and placement

3A

3B

3C

And once Jessica was happy with the final cover, I mocked up paperback visuals which include a spine and back cover using the landscape images you saw earlier.

Stage 4 - visualising the paperback cover

Until we had a finished design. Of course there are more steps and more emails back and forth in between, but essentially this is the process. Some covers take longer than others, some require more visuals, some less. It depends on the author and the cover.

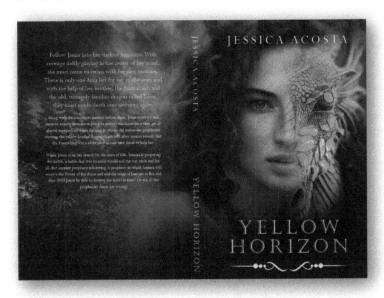

Finalising the paperback

When it comes to finalising your paperback cover there's a few more things a designer will need to get your artwork print-ready. They'll need your final blurb, and other elements you've decided you want on your cover such as publisher logo if you have one, web address, RRP and so on.

They'll also need to know which printer you have decided to

use because requirements for print-ready files vary slightly printer to printer. Essentially you'll be asked for your final book size (e.g. 5 x 8", 5.5 x 8.5" etc.), your paper type (e.g. white or cream) and your final page count (unless you are commissioning your cover designer to also format your interior, in which case they will know this once they have completed the interior).

The paper type and page count will determine the spine width. And the choice of printer can affect the paper type too. The paper used by one printer can be greater in weight or bulk than another printer, for example. Some printers will also have a choice of paper weights and types.

Which brings me on to a common question …

White or cream paper?

This depends on the book, the subject matter and other factors, but as a general rule white paper for non-fiction and cream paper for fiction.

White paper for fiction looks cheap and nasty and shrieks amateur.

To Summarise:

- Supply your designer with blurb, outline, descriptions of elements or scenes you see working on the cover as well as cover contents such as title and author name

- Research a handful of covers in your genre that you like

- Always opt for cream paper for fiction interior, and potentially white for non-fiction

Chapter 7
Making a Decision

Some people know what they like and are very decisive, other people aren't as confident in their own decisions. Your designer will be able to steer you in the direction they believe is right, and you can ask for the opinions of friends and family, but ultimately the decision is yours.

You have spent hours, months, years, writing and editing and writing and editing, and you're finally reaching the point of publishing and what a lot of people feel is the fun part of the process – designing your cover. But by the very nature of the book being your own, you're too close to the book and have had fixed ideas for too long as to what you think the cover should look like.

This is a common problem and one of the reasons I send people off to look at covers in their genre – it sparks ideas, and opens people's minds to what is out there and what is selling well.

Some authors are more than happy to give a design the thumbs-up, do a cover reveal, and tell their friends, family and followers that this is the cover for their latest release. Those people know what they like and they know their market. They believe in the process we've been through and are confident the cover will sell.

Other authors say: 'I like this one, do you agree?' Sometimes I do, sometimes I don't. I'll give an honest answer to the question and if I think another design was stronger I'll say so. Sometimes they'll stick to their guns and go with the one they like, and the rest of the time they go and ask other people for confirmation.

Your friends and family are <u>not</u> the best people to ask

Friends and family are great, they are supportive and keen and want you to be happy and fulfilled in your writing career. They are even excited that you're publishing a new book. But they aren't the right people to ask for an opinion unless they are your target market. You need to ask people who read the kind of books that you write. I wouldn't dream of asking my husband or my brother what they thought of a bunch of steamy romance novel covers. What appeals to one fan base, won't appeal to another.

Impulse buy versus critique

When you ask your readership which cover they prefer, generally speaking they will look long and hard at your cover and critique it. They'll have an opinion on the model you've used, the font size, or the colours. Their opinion isn't a true test of the power of impulse buying.

Everyone has an opinion

Especially writers. Writers are used to critiquing each other's work, and that leads to a lot of opinions. Given that most opinions are sought via the internet, people are braver about being ruthless and saying exactly what they think of something without a second thought as to how helpful or valid their opinion is. The other problem is there are a lot of 'experts' out there. People who have 'been in the industry for so many years', etc. That's great, and sometimes those people will have very valid opinions, but other times they'll just regurgitate general industry opinion, such as 'the title must be as large as possible, until it's filled the entire cover and you can't see anything but the title' – an exaggeration, but you get the idea. The principles behind what they are saying are usually sound, but don't necessarily apply to every genre, or trend, or what will actually work and sell your book. They just want to sound like they know what they're talking about.

Designed by Committee

The problem with a committee is that lots of opinions don't make for a single clear vision. I've seen a lot of 'cover design workshops' happening online where an author will post up a mediocre cover or several variations of mediocre covers they've either done themselves or they've asked a designer to do, and then all their Facebook friends have waded in with how to make the cover better, and they've had the cover tweaked and pulled in various different directions. In the end it'll look a bit different but it won't look better – it might even look worse. Asking opinions won't make it better unless you happen to get the opinion of a great cover designer.

Turn feedback into publicity

One of the great things about posting visuals and asking for feedback when you have a growing fanbase is that it's an excuse for reader interaction. So long as you don't take the feedback to heart or too seriously (writers have enough to cope with in reading reviews of their books!). It's a way of engaging your audience and making them feel a part of the process of creating your book.

To Conclude:

If you've asked a designer to work on your covers and you have a few really great and striking options to choose from, then ask a few readers of your specific genre which cover they like best. If you ask them, you'll usually see a pattern of which they think will work best for your market, and if they read heavily in your market they are probably right.

However, if you've employed a cheap designer, or done them yourself, you're not going to do yourself any favours asking people to choose between a range of mediocre covers.

If you're unsure, change the author name on your cover so it's not your own, then put it alongside some traditionally published book covers, and ask a group of readers in the genre which covers they like best and why. You'll soon see a pattern emerge if your cover is never mentioned.

Chapter 8
Other Book Cover Requirements

Designing a series

Books in a series need to look like part of a set. There are various ways of achieving this, from using the same fonts, or colours, perhaps a particular layout or style of image. Maybe it's one or all of these things. It's worth bearing in mind when the first is being designed how the others might work as part of the set.

Here's an example of a series rebrand I did for Joanna Penn, thriller writer, www.JFPenn.com. She wanted them to really stand out, whilst using key elements that sell thrillers (the running figures). You'll notice there's a lot going on in each image, but with the titles bold and white, the author name bright in yellow, and each cover having a strong colour theme, they really stand out.

 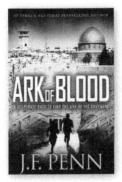 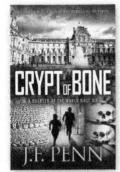

3D Covers

It looks really smart on websites and publicity material to have a 3D cover. You can either have a designer create you a bespoke 3D cover exactly to your requirements, or there are also cover creation tools available such as http://boxshot.com/3d-pack/ which work well.

Box Sets

You've written a series and you want to market them together in a box set. Again, you can have your designer create one, or you can try your hand at making one yourself in free software (I haven't managed to find a decent box set tool).

One thing you need to consider is legibility of the wording on the front and spines, because with the distorting of the cover for perspective, you start to lose legibility.

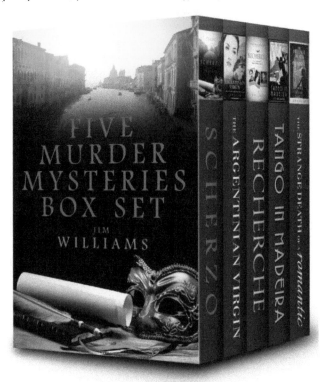

There is also the added problem that this is the norm for box set artwork, with the 3D render being on a white background. It appeals to readers because they instantly expect more than one book. However, Apple won't allow 3D books, but after debate with Smashwords, who distribute to Apple, I managed to gain approval on the cover below.

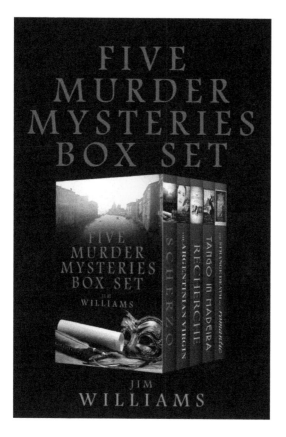

As long as the title and author name are shown in 2D, then they'll allow the 3D image to be included on the cover also.

Chapter 9

Not Just the Cover
- FORMATTING

The cover isn't the only part of a book which is important. *Quality* formatting (typesetting) is equally essential. Good formatting can be both consciously and subconsciously picked up on by readers and book buyers alike. Bad formatting is as damning as bad proofreading – reviewers are only too happy to mention it in their reviews.

Formatting and typesetting – what's the difference?

Many authors are confused by the terms *formatting [type]* and *typesetting*. They are in fact the same thing, from letter-press through to digital.

> *From Wiki: Typesetting is the composition of text by means of arranging physical types or the digital equivalents. Stored letters and other symbols (called sorts in mechanical systems and glyphs in digital systems) are retrieved and ordered according to a language's orthography for visual display.*

Formatting is the same as copy editing, right? Wrong.

I've been asked a few times if formatting includes copy editing or proofreading. It doesn't; it's not the same thing and can't be done simultaneously. Copy editing is done by a copy editor, whereby they physically edit your manuscript or text, tightening sentences, suggesting improvements, making structural changes, depending on the type of copy editing you have asked for or need. This should be done before proofreading or formatting.

Proofreading is done by a proofreader. Sometimes this might be the same person who copy edited depending on the breadth of their skillset, sometimes it may be done by someone who specialises in proofreading. This is checking for spelling errors, consistency, and in the latter stages formatting errors. Either way, before submitting a manuscript to your formatter/typesetter, you should have made sure that you are absolutely happy with everything in the manuscript, and that it has been proofread by another person thoroughly.

Then, and only then, should you hand it over to be formatted.

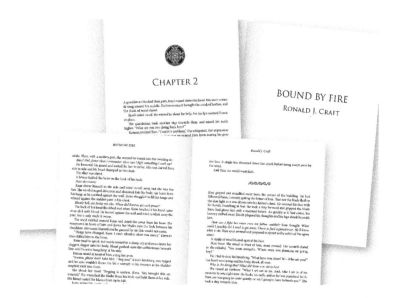

Any formatter/designer will send proofs back to you to check over, and it's normal for them to include two sets of amendments within their quotation. Some may stipulate how many amendments are included, but you would need to check this with the individual. These amendments should generally be in addition to any formatting errors they may have made.

Supplying your manuscript

Generally a Microsoft Word document is preferable to supplying files in any other format, as your formatter will be able to open it up easily. It's also easier and more straightforward (with less likelihood for formatting errors) if your document is clean. For example, setting paragraph indents using the paragraph indent box, and not by using several taps of the space bar, because your typesetter will potentially feel suicidal if you do.

It's best to remain consistent throughout, and stick to popular fonts for your draft, such as Times or Arial, which can then be easily formatted by your typesetter to match, for example, the fonts used on the cover, to maintain consistency and an overall style.

All of these elements make for a stress-free experience for both you, the author, and for your formatter, and it therefore keeps costs down.

Don't worry about the document page size, page numbers, running headers or font sizes being a bit askew. Your formatter will sort all that out.

Whatever you do, don't:

- Write like you're using a typewriter and hit return at the end of a line (only do this to start a new paragraph). This is really important as it's not something that is easy to remedy.

- Put two spaces between a period and the start of a new sentence. Computer software handles a slightly larger space these days, and if you double space you end up with really large gaps in fully justified text. If you have, don't worry, it's easy enough to find/replace a double space with a single one.

- Put a return between every paragraph to create a gap between them like this book. Use the Paragraph dialogue box to dictate a 'space after'. 10-20pt is usually adequate and can be globally changed if required.

- Hit the space bar several times to create an indent! Use the Paragraph dialogue box to create a First Line Indent.

Keeping costs down

It's possible for books to be formatted, review copies printed and sent out, the book then edited some more, whole sections deleted, before having it proofread again, edited again, proofread again, formatted again, proofread several more times … you get the idea … but this is a costly process. All this can be minimised by making sure the book is thoroughly edited and proofread before it is formatted. It also saves a lot of work for yourself as well. The alternative would be to format yourself if you know you're a meddler and will want to keep making changes.

Personally, I always format the first chapter or two of a book before formatting the whole manuscript. This means things can be tweaked and changed such as fonts and margins and chapter headings and so on easily first, then the agreed-upon format can be rolled out throughout the rest of the book.

The reason that authors should make sure they're happy with everything is that it is time-consuming and therefore costly to transpose any errors onto the typesetter's file, which for paperback printing are generally produced in either Adobe InDesign or Quark, professional design software, rather than Word.

It can also be cheaper to have the ebook and paperback versions done at the same time.

Formatting yourself

With any formatting, whether it's paperback or ebook, there are problems which can arise. Firstly, when individual authors come to format their own book, it's not something they do on a regular basis. Formatting is not only a professional occupation, but it also takes time to learn how to do it properly. I've seen authors battle to format their book, and even when they're finished, the end product still looks amateur.

Many people can and do format their own books and manage to achieve an acceptable standard. Out of cover design and formatting, the latter is the one I would suggest an author tackle themselves should their budget not stretch to both. It's the easier of the two and although professional formatting can make a difference, it's more straightforward to make your interior look good than your cover if you follow the basic rules of formatting.

What many people don't understand is that even if the book looks okay, there are tell-tale signs which if not consciously, then subconsciously, readers and/or book buyers will pick up.

Common formatting mistakes

Text too small or too big

This isn't a problem in ebooks, because readers can adjust the size of text to suit their preference. But in paperbacks many authors make the text too small to save on page count and thus decrease the cost of book printing, and readers strain to read, meaning they'll put the book down.

A friend of mine once said to me that he gave up on a book because there were *too many words on the page and that he didn't feel he was getting anywhere reading the book, or making progress.* It's funny. Because the text on each page was both small and the margins tiny, he psychologically felt that he was treading water, rather than swimming.

On the other extreme, most authors actually make their text too large, or line spacing increased too much, and it means the book is bigger and more expensive to produce, leaving little profit. 11pt is about right for a paperback, give or take.

Margins and gutters

Incorrect margins or gutters can also affect a paperback page count, and more worrying is when there is no gutter on the book and text runs too close to the spine, meaning it's difficult to read.

Page numbering

Page numbers starting on the title page, on the front matter, and on blank pages really lets a book down. They should ideally start chapter one, and be omitted on blank pages. For example, if every chapter starts on a right-hand-facing page (which is a preference and not essential), then there will be occasional blank left-hand-facing pages. These should not display a page number.

Ebooks do not have page numbers, they have locations. This is determined by the e-reading device and not by the formatter.

Fonts

Fonts for paperback interiors should be easy on the eye. Those used most in formatting text-heavy pages are chosen specifically because they are easy to read. Choose the wrong font and your readers could have a headache before the end of the first chapter.

My favourite fonts for formatting paperbacks are: Minion Pro, Adobe Caslon Pro, Adobe Garamond Pro. Other options are: Janson, Bembo and Baskerville.

And if you're formatting non-fiction you might consider a sans-serif font (i.e. without tails): Futura, Franklin Gothic, Helvetica, Myriad.

The exception is the title page, and if possible should reflect or be sympathetic to the cover design, and you can also use the fonts from the cover for chapter headings.

Good/Bad formatting

Text too big/too small, bad font choice, incorrect gutters, bad indents, page numbering blank pages or title pages, random blank pages, unjustified paragraphs

Header and page numbering too large and body text too small

Gutter and margins too small – difficult to read on paperback

Indents too large and inconsistent

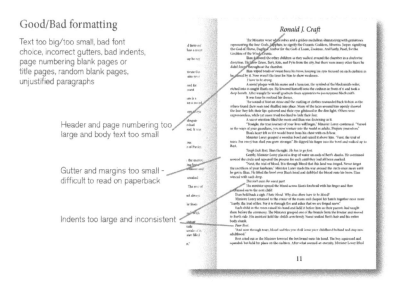

Above is an example of bad formatting, with the mistakes marked. Below is the same book well-formatted. Can you see the difference?

Exporting print-ready files

This is where paperback formatting is slightly easier than cover design. Lots of places accept Word documents, but people do have problems with fonts embedding, and unless you've got a secure PDF file to upload, things wobble and change and don't necessary turn out as you expected on the printed proof. But that's what proofs are for … checking to make sure everything is as it should be.

Keeping things simple

Ebooks bring their own set of problems that print books don't have. Requirements are changing every day. The best advice is to keep things simple, particularly if you're producing fiction and you don't need a fixed layout or images and tables and graphs and so on. The simpler and cleaner the file you upload to Amazon Kindle, Smashwords, Kobo, etc., the more likely it is to work across multiple platforms, on various devices, now and in the future. Bear in mind lots of people have older devices, and books need to work on those too.

Checking your proofs

Regardless of where you choose, who you choose, and what format you have your book produced in, whether ebook or print book, it goes without saying that you should, absolutely, 100%, once the book has been formatted, check the entire book thoroughly before making it available to purchase.

You don't want your first review to be a bad one.

To Summarise:

- Formatting and typesetting are the same thing

- Formatting is not copy editing or proofreading

- Make sure you have your manuscript properly edited and proofread BEFORE formatting

- Avoid common formatting mistakes if DIY

- Paperback and ebook formatting is not the same

- Check your proofs AFTER formatting to make sure nothing has gone awry.

Chapter 10

Supplementary Design Considerations

Marketing Materials

Other design considerations consist, generally, of marketing materials.

Bookmarks

Bookmarks are a really great accompaniment to take to signings, promotional fairs, simply to have in your bag for when you meet someone interested in your books, to post out with a message when you send books out for review or for direct orders.

I'd recommend having them matte laminated, as they are something people use and reuse and the lamination makes them more durable.

www.stressfreeprint.co.uk/bookmarks (UK)

www.vistaprint.com (US)

Flyers

Weirdly, you can get flyers printed much cheaper than bookmarks. Remember that in the UK, if you order a flyer and it doesn't contain an 'offer' or a discount, it's not eligible for VAT (value added tax) so you can save yourself a whopping 20%. Printed.com are an excellent value and also have some lovely templates if you want to create your own flyers.

www.printed.com/products/4/leaflets--flyers

Posters

Posters are useful for advertising signings in bookshop windows, and if you have one designed for a space to add dates and times you can have a few printed at the same time and use them for different events.

www.stressfreeprint.co.uk/bookmarks (UK)

www.vistaprint.com (US)

Roller Banners

These are great at events such as book signings or launch parties. I recently designed one for the Triskele Books launch party with the logo printed like wallpaper so people could have their photo taken in front of it like at the awards. It cost about £35, including the carry bag, from here:

www.rollerbannersuk.com

Advertising

There's also advertising, both in print and online, for which you might need adverts designing. Sometimes these can be produced for free by the publication and they'll ask you for copy and images, or you might want the designer who created your book cover to do this for you.

Online presence

There are also various online networks that you will need to maximise graphically – places such as your Facebook profile picture and page or group banner. Banner adverts on other websites. Not to mention your website …

What to include

I thought I would touch on the subject of **what** you might include on marketing materials and printed promotion as so many people ask, and when you're stepping into the world of self-promotion for the first time it can be a little scary. It's not normally in a designer's remit to come up with the content for your cover or materials, but I've seen a lot of content in my time so I'll share some tips.

Firstly, it's not always essential to include a picture of your book on marketing materials, although it needs to be clear that that is what you are promoting, to avoid any confusion. A strapline (or one-liner) works well on the fronts of book covers and also on the promotional items that are either small or are only going to be seen at a glance, whereas on postcards and websites, etc., you may consider using a full blurb. Quotes from famous authors, or those whose reputation in your genre is known, can be useful.

QR codes – a barcode that is scannable on your phone to take you to a specific web address (i.e. your Amazon sales page or website) – are commonly used on printed items and can be generated online free. Everything you include has one of two purposes – to entice people to buy or find out more, or to give them information on where they can buy or find out more.

Lastly, and this is becoming more common the more I see groups of authors collaborating, forming collectives or indie imprints, is to create a logo and a 'look' for the group. This doesn't mean all of the covers have to look the same, in the same way that in a major publishing house all the covers under one imprint don't look the same. But what it does mean is that a generic logo and ident (such as Penguin's penguin) can be used on each book within the imprint, labelling books as being part of a larger group and what that group stands for, or in the case of individual authors, many want to give the impression of being published by a 'Publisher', and so create the publisher themselves and brand their books as such. This can give the impression of books being published professionally, by a publisher, rather than self-published by an individual.

Chapter 11
Budget

One of the main concerns when it comes to publishing your own work is the expense. You want to do it right so you know you need a copy editor, proofreader, cover designer and formatter. You might even be considering engaging a publicist. How much should you budget for cover design and formatting?

Major publishers are known to spend anywhere from £500 - £3000 on a book cover, more in some instances, but that's not necessary for an author self-publishing.

Realistically, I would set a budget of around £100 - £500 depending on the quality and experience of the cover designer, and around £10 - £30 for stock imagery depending on where you source your images and how many you end up using.

Here are some examples of covers designed by freelance designers for independent authors:

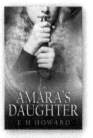

Chapter 12
The Current Marketplace

Since the early days of Amazon Kindle, it's never been harder to get your book noticed and find new readers than it is today. Amazon made self-publishing easy, and other ebook retailers followed, and that means the market is swamped with books of varying quality.

Where once a mediocre cover was enough to secure reasonable sales, it's not so simple any more, and the marketplace has become much more competitive. Authors and publishers alike know they have to package their books to appeal to their readership, and one of the ways of doing that is to ensure their book covers are as good as if not better than the bestselling books in their genre.

Your book cover won't just be on a retailer's website, but on Facebook and Twitter profiles, on Goodreads and review sites, websites and other marketing collateral. It is the face of a book and a huge part of an author's brand.

A design glossary and case studies follow, but before you move on, I'd like to leave you with something one of my bestselling clients said to me when I first took over designing their book covers …

"By the way, sales have doubled since your wonderful new covers went live." Fenella Miller

Chapter 13
Branding

Back in 2011, traditional publishing was playing it safe and no one was prepared to take a risk on an unknown writer. The alternative, self-publishing, was beginning to gain ground, but still appeared to be full of poorly written, unedited vanity projects with home-made covers. Plus, the huge amount of effort required to market the book seemed an impossible task.

Gillian Hamer, JJ Marsh and Liza Perrat met in London to discuss their options. The idea surfaced of a team effort. Going the independent route, together, seemed more man-ageable. They talked honestly about their fears of failure and inadequacies as marketers. They established their ideals – high quality writing and professional presentation.

I had known all three for some years via various online writing sites. At this point I was not a cover designer but worked for a brand agency. They came to me to ask if I would brand their author collective. At the time the term *author collective* was new in the fast-changing world of publishing.

Sure, I said. And so we set off on our journey together which would see the growth of a successful indie collective.

But what is brand?

Brand is **everything**.

You can take that two ways. Firstly, brand is important. And you can also take it to mean that brand is all-encompassing. They are intrinsically connected.

For authors, brand is everything from your narrative voice and the subjects you deal with and the way you deal with them, to the standard of your proofreading and the physical quality of your paperbacks. It's how you speak at events, the way you engage with readers on social media, and how you reply to fan mail. It's how you dress and the way you present yourself, it's where you write, be it a café or a garden shed, it's all the little things that build up a picture of you and your personality. It is literally everything you do to present yourself and your work, reflecting you as an author.

It's your reputation, a reader's assumption, a path you want to take, and how you wish to be perceived. You might want to be perceived as loud and breaking the boundaries of literature, rebelling against the rules of the English language; or you might want to be a recluse, someone who attends literary events to quietly share their passion. Either would be reflected in the work of the person, from their jacket covers to their personality when you meet them. Rule-breaking would be accepted if not expected of the former, whereas frowned upon in the latter. But that's okay, so long as the brand focuses on what's being delivered.

For Gillian, JJ and Liza, not only did brand encompass each of them as authors, but their collective as a whole. If one person within the collective chose to have sub-standard editing done on their manuscript, it would reflect upon the group as a whole, damaging the brand they were keen to build. So it was important they agreed how they wanted to present themselves.

The quality of their proofreading, editing and so on was up to them. My remit was to create a logo, website, and blog, and to design their covers and format their books to a quality standard. I would go on to create postcards, banners, bookmarks and business cards. The idea behind the styling was to create a recognisable look and feel which would be synonymous with quality fiction and cutting-edge independent publishing.

To date they have published nineteen books between them.

"Triskele Books stands on three legs: a strong sense of place, high-quality writing and professional presentation. The first two we could handle by ourselves. Yet design? We had to get this right from the start and ensure a distinctive identity. Clear, simple, reflective of our ethos and flexible enough to grow with us.

"An odd seaweed-like ornament on someone's mantelpiece suggested the triskele, a Celtic symbol of individuality balanced with support. Perfect.

"Jane supplied us with a selection of images, a range of colours and artwork to fit all our publicity materials. Five years on, after all our changes, it still works. Because we got it right first time." – JJ Marsh

Appendix I
Case Studies

Kristin Gleeson, *Raven Brought the Light*

www.kristingleeson.com

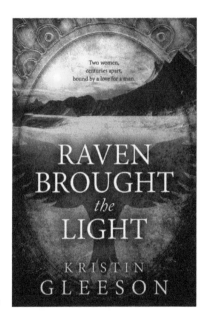

As an artist myself I love to look at well-designed book covers and understand the importance of a good cover. I do know that I am not a designer and that skill and talent is different to an artist, but though I may not be able to do it, I feel I have a good idea of what will sell and what is a good design for the kind of books I write.

When my first books were published, a novel and a biography, I was under contract with traditional publishers and I had very little say in the book covers. The novel, *Selkie Dreams*, was set in Alaska and, in the panhandle where there was a temperate rainforest, totem poles and huge snow-capped mountains and loads of seals. It was based around the myth of humans transformed into seals. The first image I was shown contained a bleak landscape from the arctic with a glacier in the distance. In the end I provided my own photographs and had a better result.

When I went indie a few years later the first cover designer I used was happy to have input, but the designer had difficulty translating the input into a satisfactory result. I sent sample covers of books in my genre, I gave sample images and photographs, but the result in my view was unsatisfactory. The figures looked fake and poorly Photoshopped, the colour was off, the font was boring or not suited to the genre. Each time I went back with my criticisms and changes I would be charged. It was a small enough fee, but it was annoying because I felt they hadn't listened to me in the first place. I went with one of their covers eventually, but searched around for a better designer. It was a few months later that I found Jane and the difference was astronomical. She understood my desire for a look, a brand that was me and a brand for each series that I created. I pulled down my book and as soon as she had the new design for the book (*Along the Far Shore*) I put it back up. What a huge difference. I'd had only a handful of sales before that, but with the new cover I began to notice a real change in sales. I know it's down to her cover designs that I secured a review in a national newspaper for my latest book and had interest from a national book chain.

Anne Stormont, author of *Change of Life*

www.annestormont.co.uk

A Personal Account:

As the saying goes, it's important you 'don't judge a book by its cover.' It's a noble sentiment. However, in its literal sense when specifically applied to books, most book buyers probably do base their decision to purchase on the appeal of the cover. So authors getting the cover of their books right is crucial if they're going to hook their prospective readers.

When I began writing my first novel in 2005, I hadn't given the cover of the finished product any thought. But at the end of 2009, with the novel completed, and having taken the decision to go down the indie route to publication, I was forced to start thinking about it.

'Didn't know where to start' is an understatement. Oh, I knew I wanted a first-class, professional cover. I'd spent money on having the book professionally edited and proofread and I wasn't going to skimp on the cover. I understood the importance of a good cover. I knew that getting it right required talent and skill. I appreciated that the process of coming up with a good visual design is both complex and subtle.

I also grasped the significance of the visual, nowadays more than ever, in grabbing people's attention. I could see that even for an ebook a good cover is important. Online booksellers like Amazon still need to present a cover image in their shop window. I could even see that the cover would therefore have to look equally as good in the virtual thumbnail world as well as in the real world.

And I had some vague idea of how I'd like the cover to look. I also definitely knew what I didn't want.

BUT knowing and accepting all of the above didn't mean I could design my own cover. So the search was on.

I went down the word-of-mouth and evidence of my own eyes route. I'd bought the books of a couple of other indie-published authors and was impressed by the covers. I contacted these authors through an online writers' forum we all belonged to and they told me about Jane Dixon Smith, who as a writer herself was also on the forum.

I didn't need to approach anyone else once Jane and I made contact. We got along from the start. Jane was easily approachable and friendly. I sent her a brief synopsis of the novel, the back cover blurb and the word count. I also had to come up with a strapline, after Jane had explained to me what one of those was.

Her fees were reasonable and within my budget. And, after a few emails back and forth, which included me outlining my vague and feeble ideas for what I might like incorporated in the cover, Jane had come up with two or three designs for me to consider. These included various fonts and positions for the book title and the author name, as well as (for the paperback version) the back cover look and layout and what would be on the spine.

I should say I also engaged Jane's services to design the interior of the book and convert it for uploading in all the required file versions for various publishing platforms. This was something that for me would have been just as daunting as cover design. So I ended up with everything ready in all the various and correct formats and all I had to do was press publish.

I was delighted with the finished article. My book looked good – more than good enough to be judged by its cover.

In 2014 I published my second novel. I didn't hesitate to approach Jane again. Second time around I had a slightly clearer idea of the elements I'd like included. By then I knew about stock photos and lightboxes. I was able to share images I liked with Jane, but again I'd no idea how to design a finished look. And again the process was entirely done by email and was quick and painless. I love the cover of my second novel even more than the first. It's been complimented by readers, booksellers and reviewers. At the same time as publishing the second novel, I wanted to tweak the design of my first novel to incorporate my indie-publishing logo (also designed by Jane) on the spine and to give the two books a similar 'corporate look' inside and out. This was no problem to Jane and again I was happy with the outcome.

And my most recent commission for Jane was last year when I published my first novel for children. The process was the same as before – email consultation, me providing a lightbox of possible elements as a starting point along with the book's vital statistics, price agreed upfront for paperback and ebook versions, and to include interior formatting. Again I received a few possible cover versions for consideration and modification. A couple more emails and suggestions/discussions, and once again the end result was a great cover.

In summary then, choosing and working with a book/cover designer was quick, painless and most definitely worth the money. I worked hard on my books. I'm proud of them and love them unconditionally. But I wrote them to be read, not necessarily to make money, but definitely to be read. And so, as well as investing my time in the writing, I view it as equally important to invest time and money in finding and employing a good designer to give my books the best chance of appealing to readers as they cast their eye along the bookshop shelf or down the online page.

I don't have the necessary talent or knowledge to design a book cover, so I hired the services of someone who does. It was for the same reasons that I hired an editor and a proof-reader. I want to be seen as a professional writer and publisher who produces professional quality goods.

My books are worth it, I'm worth it. It's a no-brainer.

Eric Tomlinson, author of *Amara's Daughter*

www.ozcreative.co.uk

How does the ant catch the elephant's eye?

So, I wrote a book. Over three years of my life I'll never see again. I might never get rich, but I really want people to read it, give feedback and hopefully appreciate my work.

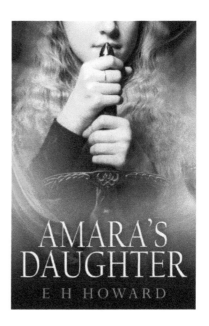

My first book was non-fiction. I knew what I wanted on the cover, but didn't have a clue how to get it. So, I bought a "teach yourself to draw" book and knocked something together.

Older, wiser and more informed, when I came to release my first fiction book, I knew I wanted a good cover, but didn't have a clue how to get it.

There's an entire industry waiting to rip off the wide-eyed writer: editors, agents, proofreaders and designers. For every one that will do the job they're paid for, it feels like there are a dozen more ready to take the cash and never deliver.

What is the purpose of the cover?

It's great to imagine a row of books standing at the airport waiting to be plucked up by the travelling masses, but reality is my books are unlikely to ever stand in a bookshop in pristine rows. They might make the secondhand/charity shop, but not the airport lounge.

My books are going to sell as ebooks. Which means they're going to be browsed on a phone/iPad/webpage. Often, they're going to be the size of a thumbnail.

How does the ant catch the elephant's eye?

Although I didn't realise it at the time, the cover is also part of a brand. Sounds grandiose, but most ebooks are read as part of a series. There needs to be a common style suitable for subsequent books. When the potential reader sees the new book in thumbnail, they need to mentally associate it with the last one.

I was nervous of approaching a professional company. I didn't think they'd be interested in discussing my pathetic little book. Or, if they gushed over how wonderful it was, I'd know they were sharks out to rip me off.

I've been in business for thirty years and I know when a customer says price doesn't matter, they're out of their depth and haven't a clue; of course price matters. I can't justify spending a large amount on what my wife already sees as a complete waste of time.

I know writers who go against their better judgement seem to always regret it. So, I needed to be part of the process. However, as a program designer, I know each time the client changes their mind it costs time and money. A graphic designer is the same. The only asset they have is their ability, sold in units of time. I think my biggest fear was ending up with a huge bill because I kept dithering and changing my mind.

I realise now that what I needed was a mentor to guide me through the design process. Somebody I could trust to nudge me towards colours and images without dominating the project with their choice. The cover had to remain mine. Almost as personal as if I had drawn it, but … better.

An email discussion placed the price as acceptable and the assurance of reworking the images until I was happy seemed more than generous. I had no idea about colours, images or branding.

Much more subtle, I thought in terms of a single image. Where a 'real' designer thinks in terms of blending multiple images to create the final artwork.

For me, this is one of the key indicators for a professional cover: it's artwork, not a picture. There are thousands of books with pictures on the cover.

When book two came to fruition, the final cover design fitted perfectly with the first, that wasn't by any plan of mine. It's a no-brainer where I'll go for cover number three.

The way I see it, I have around half a second to attract attention to my tiny portion of the potential reader's screen. And yes, I'm selling. I honestly believe that great artwork is the only way I'm going to do that. Sure, the book is great, but who doesn't judge a book by its cover?

Jan Ruth, author of *Midnight Sky*

www.janruth.com

I was at a crossroads three years ago, wondering whether to take the plunge and approach a designer to tackle my lack of theme and 'branding'. Self-publishing allows the author to make all the decisions, but I didn't have the required skills to implement this process to a satisfactory

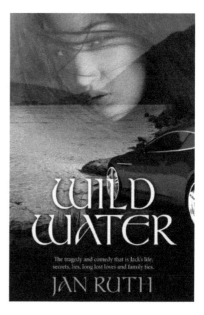

level, not only from a practical point of view but also from an emotive point of view. I might know the material inside-out but could I make the right decision from a commercial point of view?

I've always been committed to constantly improving, striving to produce that quality product – so the natural progression was to have professional covers which represented the content. I was initially wary, as I'd seen all kinds of inferior work, and my first novel, *Wild Water*, was perhaps the most difficult to represent in terms of content and genre. I guess it's a contemporary romance with mature characters, a blend of tragic-comedy. My other notable theme is that of setting, which I'm very strong on in terms of writing.

Initially, I sourced images which resonated with me, concentrating on just two or three elements. The lake background was a natural starting point.

I sent these on to the designer, and then we got to work.

I was presented with three or four mock-ups for *Wild Water*. I was thrilled with her initial idea; that of floating the woman's face above the water. Merging her into the lake had the character look cemented into the landscape, and this is exactly right for my material. I would never have thought of this. The blending technique added a sense of loneliness, beauty and angst. Two other points which I hadn't considered were the choice of font – an important and often overlooked aspect of cover design – and the way the cover looked as a tiny thumbprint on the Internet.

As we moved through the various tweaking stages, I could see where this theme would work across further novels. *Wild Water* has since developed into a series, and that initial branding was so important to get right because it's made the follow-on books not only easier to design, but they all work hard to tell the story at a glance …

Working with a freelance designer on your book cover is a bespoke service. No one knows your material as well as you do, but you might not be the person to pull it all together.

Lorna Fergusson, author of *The Chase* and *Informed with Other Passions*

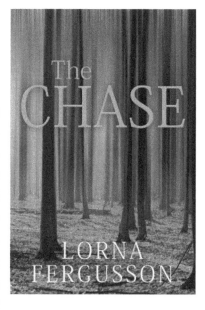

I'm one of those authors who had already experienced traditional publishing – and I was a lucky one too, because my novel *The Chase* was originally published by Bloomsbury. I remember thinking at the time that I was in safe hands in terms of the cover design. All the same, I couldn't help feeling it would be useful to come up with a set of design ideas, so I provided cover images for novels by Carol McGrath and Tracy Chevalier.

When it came to the paperback jacket I had no input – I was told they wanted to take a different, more mass market approach. Thankfully, the image they used was gorgeous once again – a haunting, atmospheric woodland in shades of spring green.

Scroll on a few years and in the wake of the new wave of self-publishing, I retrieved the rights to *The Chase* with a view to bringing it out myself. I knew I couldn't use the previous covers and I was concerned that the novel should look as good as possible. I started looking – really looking – at jacket images. What did they say about subject and genre? How did they catch the eye? How did they work at thumbnail size, or in black and white? I started checking out names of designers whose work appealed to me. I approached one or two and soon found Jane Dixon-Smith of JD Smith Design, embarking on what has been a very pleasurable and fulfilling process.

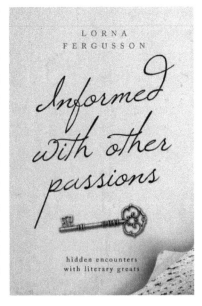

LORNA FERGUSSON

Informed with other passions

hidden encounters with literary greats

How did that process work? For anyone who wants to work with a designer, research is crucial. Not only should you research potential designers, looking at the range of work in their portfolios and any testimonials they have, but make sure you're both clear in correspondence prior to agreement just what it is you want. For me it was important to feel I'd have input and feedback and that the design could be adjusted with two-way discussion, through iterations, until I was happy.

I felt that the best way to help the designer produce the kind of design I wanted was to be very clear in my brief to her. I sent Jane a summary of the novel, key scenes and images, the kind of readership it would have and comparison novels in the market. (*The Chase* has been likened both to Daphne du Maurier and Joanne Harris). Self-publishing writers need to know what their category is and how images can predispose the reader to see the story as sitting within a particular genre.

The brief included references to cover designs I'd admired, sample taglines – including 'The past will hunt you down' which we eventually used - and a list of potential cover notions. These included a mysterious woodland scene, Perigordine architecture, cave paintings, tapestries, and so on.

Jane came up with an excellent selection of images too and we started the process of focussing in on what I actually wanted. She sent through some possible treatments, including pictures of pathways through woodlands and a castle above woods. Tapestries didn't work, cave painting images I liked had appeared in other covers – this is something to watch out for. If everyone is using the same photo libraries, the same images come up again and again. You may have noticed this in mainstream publishing as well.

Some images were truly gorgeous but we decided against them because the details were too subtle and this meant they didn't work well at thumbnail size. As *The Chase* was going to appear as an ebook before being a paperback, that thumbnail really mattered.

Eventually, I tracked down the woodland image we used in the end. I loved it because it was mysterious, striking and unusual, in orange tones rather that the expected green. Its vibrant colour 'popped' off the screen.

You may think of jackets in terms of images, but a cover design is so much more than that. It's all about how the designer manipulates or adapts that image. It's about the placing of elements on the page. And it's about the typography. So many people forget about this, yet when an independently published cover is criticised as being amateur, it's often because of poor choice of font plus inadequate placing and kerning of the lettering.

Jane sent through sets of sample fonts which, as with the cover image, were refined down from six options, to three, to one. Then it was about the placing: to have the title at the top, midway, below or above my name. Placement of the tagline. Proportions of title to author name. Colour of title. We both liked the title in gold against the tawny forest, but for the ebook I chose white for the title, simply because it stood out more.

At every stage, I shrank the image down to thumbnail and also made it monochrome, to check for interest and clarity.

Later, once I'd decided to produce the paperback, Jane extended the image and I composed the blurb. She also designed my Fictionfire Press logo, did all the formatting and produced beautiful publicity postcards.

I was so happy with all this that I have commissioned Jane to produce a cover for my next book, *Informed with Other Passions*. The brief was easier this time: a collection of historical short stories about literary figures seen from unusual perspectives. I asked her to select from concepts of secrets, manuscripts, locks, boxes, paper, keys, sealing wax.

She produced three several suggestions – they were all so brilliant I had a hard time deciding! The one I've gone for has a beautiful and eye-catching font imitating script, plus an ornate key and a curled sheet revealing a handwritten script beneath. It lures you in to find out more. Once again, we negotiated the typography and checked it all for readability and visual impact.

What have I learnt from this process? I've learnt that it's important to find the right designer whom you can trust, who is flexible, creative, professional, efficient and prompt. It's crucial to give the designer assistance where you can with suggested images and a clear brief, along with a sense of genre and market, but it's also important to allow the designer to bring their own ideas and concepts to the project.

Think of your cover as being as much of a 'hook' as the first line or paragraph of your story. It can be quirky, beautiful, atmospheric, punchy – there must be something in it that triggers the reader's curiosity.

It must be legible at small scale, and appropriate for the type of book it is: colours, images and typography all signal what kind of book it is and which genre.

Allow the time for this process - and money. Regard your investment as well worthwhile because the right cover can really sell your book. It can say so much more than a thousand words of marketing copy. It entices the reader into turning to that first page and falling under the spell of your words.

Appendix II
Design and Print Glossary

Artwork – depending on what you're referring to, this can mean a multitude of things: 1) An illustration placed on the cover (as in a piece of art, painting, drawing, etc.); 2) A printer might refer to the finished cover design file, the print PDF, as 'artwork'; 3) Some designers refer to the process of design as 'artworking'.

Back Cover – the back cover of a printed book, generally containing blurb.

Bleed – my favourite to explain. Bleed is the image or colour which extends beyond the edge of the cover or page (normally 3mm or .0125", but occasionally 5mm or more if specified by the printer). Designers will deliberately set up cover files so that when they export a print-ready file for the publisher, there is excess image (bleed). This means that when the printer has printed your book covers and subsequently trims them (cuts them out of the large sheet on which they were printed) you do not end up with areas of cover which have no print on them. Think of it like this: if you are going to roll out pastry to line a pie dish, you roll it out larger than you need, line the pie dish, then trim off the excess. This is effectively what bleed is.

When uploading your interior to CreateSpace, you have two options for bleed. 1) Ends before the edge of the page and 2) Ends after the edge of the page. For standard fiction, where nothing touches the edge of the page, you would select *before*. If you have a book with images that touch the edge of the page, for example, you would select *after*.

Blurb – the copy on the back of your book which sells it.

Body copy/text – the bulk of text in your manuscript.

Book Size – the overall height and width of a book. E.g. 6 x 9", 5 x 8", etc.

Cover Finish – this usually refers to the type of lamination on the cover of a book. There are as standard two options with most printers: gloss or matte. When asked, I always recommend matte. It has a better quality, more luxurious feel about it. Gloss tends to look cheap and out of date.

Crop Marks (also known as registration marks, trim marks, cutting marks) – fine hairlines printed on the outer edge of your cover file. They tell the printer exactly where they need to trim/cut your cover on each edge. Some publishers add these themselves, others require the final cover files to include them (this difference between printers is fairly specific to publishing books – in the rest of the print industry it is standard to simply supply files WITH crop marks).

Drop Capitals – an enlarged letter generally used at the beginning of a chapter or section.

Fonts – the style of the characters of the alphabet. Most computers come with what are known as 'system fonts'. Many of them are good, some are recognisable as being cheap fonts that come free with software. You can download many free fonts to install on your system from the internet. These also tend to look cheap. And lastly you can also buy fonts, in much the same way as you can buy stock imagery, from websites specialising in selling fonts.

Formatting/Typesetting – generally speaking the formatting of text for the interior of a book (i.e. the words/story/prose).

Front Cover – the front cover of your book. This can be the front cover of a paperback, or the image used to display on a webpage selling an ebook.

GSM – In Europe, paper is measured in GSM. This stands for grammes/grams per square meter. And it means literally that: a sheet of paper measuring 1m x 1m = Xgsm. For example a common weight for book interiors is 80gsm.

Gutter – the gutter on a book is the margin on the inside edge of a page. It is generally larger than the margin on the outer edge of the page. The reason is that when the spine is glued, and you open a book, you would not be able to see easily any text that runs too close to the spine.

Illustration – painting, drawing (in any medium – pencil through to computer graphics) that may go on the cover or, indeed, the interior or the book. Illustration is NOT the same as cover design, and authors should be careful when employing an illustrator for their cover, that they are also a competent graphic designer, or that they are working with a graphic designer. Many graphic designers will employ an illustrator when occasion arises instead of using stock illustration or photography. Not to do a disservice to illustrators out there, but as I wouldn't take it upon myself to draw or paint something for a cover, many illustrators I have come across in my career don't have the knowledge of typography and setting files for print that a graphic designer should have.

[Image] DPI - Dots Per Inch. Think of painting an image by making lots of little dots with coloured pens. The more dots, the more complex and complete the image will look. Enough dots and you won't notice there are any dots.

[Image] Raster/Rasterised – images are either raster or vector. Rasterised images are made up of pixels/dot matrix. They're images such as photographs and any other images which has been saved down as a JPEG, TIFF and such like.

[Image] Resolution – references the quality. The higher the resolution, the better quality the image. For printed books, images are generally required to be 300 dpi at the size they are to be used. For web (i.e. images for covers of ebooks), images are only required to be around 72 dpi at the size they are to be displayed.

[Image] Vector – vector images are a designer's best friend when it comes to scalability. Rather than pixels/dots, they are made up of vectors (also known as paths or strokes), which means they can be scaled to any size imaginable. Complex graphics are made up of a series of paths and strokes that you wouldn't realise are there. These file formats can be saved as EPS or AI (Adobe Illustrator) files. Commonly they are cartoons or digital drawings, although some are so complex you wouldn't realise they are, and have a photographic quality to them.

Images of a better quality/resolution generally cost more from a stock image library than lower resolution images.

ISBN/Barcode – sometimes confused as the same thing. They are in fact two different things. An ISBN is the number allocated to books, bought from www.**isbn**.nielsenbook. co.uk (UK) or http://www.bowker.com/ (US). Some publishers buy them in bulk and sell them on or give them away free with their publishing packages. This number goes on the copyright page. On the back goes the image reference of the number, i.e. the barcode. This is an image representation of the ISBN number and usually has the number sat just below it. This is so shops can scan the book on their system, rather than having to manually input a 13-digit number. These days the barcodes are usually generated by the printer/publisher using a funky bit of software and placed on the back of the cover at the bottom (sometimes on the right-hand side) after the cover has been designed and submitted for publication. Occasionally, or if you specifically want more control over the ISBN, you can ask the publisher for the barcode, or generate your own using an online company, and have the designer place this for you.

MOBI – Kindle-specific file.

Mock Up – generally a term used for coming up with visuals of, say, a cover. Mock-up/concept/ideas/visuals.

Pantone – pantone is a range of ink colours used by the design industry. Most publishers will, however, print the interiors of books in black only, and the covers in colours made of up of Cyan, Magenta, Yellow and Black ink (CMYK).

PDF – most people have got to grips with the file format PDF these days. Most printers will require one for printing your cover and/or inside pages; others, rarely, just a high-resolution JPEG. PDF is a more secure file, which has the capability of embedding fonts and minimising anything in your file being disturbed during the printing process, whilst maintaining quality. Designers will also use them to proof your work to you. Proofing will usually be done using low-resolution (low quality), and therefore small file size, PDFs. When it comes to printing, the printer/publisher will require a high-resolution, print-ready, print-quality, PDF.

Royalty-Free Image – an image for which you pay a one-off fee to use as much as you wish, as opposed to *licensing* an image where you are limited, for example, to how many books you can have printed with the image on, and for how long (in years).

Software – Graphic Designers, for the purposes of book covers and paperback formatting, at least, use Adobe InDesign/ Quark Express, Adobe Photoshop for image manipulation, and Adobe Illustrator for manipulating or drawing vector illustrations. Anyone who actually does any formatting or page layout in Adobe Illustrator needs to seriously rethink their working practice. Kindle documents, however, are best laid out in Word and subsequently converted to MOBI files using a generator.

Spine – specific to printed books only, the spine is the part of the book where the ends of the pages are glued together. When referring to the cover, the spine is the imagery which covers the ends of the pages, typically having an author name and title on display when a book is placed on a book shelf. Designers will ask for your page count so they can calculate your spine width. This is usually done using a calculator on a publisher/printer's website, i.e. spine width = number of pages x page thickness.

Spread(s) – the left- and right-hand pages of a book which face each other is known as a 'spread' or 'facing pages'. If a designer sends you a PDF in spreads, which they potentially will when proofing a book, it means that the PDF will look as it would when you open a book, with the left- and right-hand pages next to one another as opposed to single pages.

Stock Image Library – online sites which sell images in much the same way as you can pay for and download music or software. Many of them sell Royalty-Free images.

Strapline – it's amazing how many people don't know what 'strapline' means. It's the line which goes on the front of your book which gives a further snippet as to what your book might be about (e.g. One kingdom, three brothers, three claims to the throne …)

Typography – the art of arranging type (words/titles/author name/body copy). And, yes, this does involve much more than simply centring your name and title.

A note from the author

To the world of all things design and literary I'm JD Smith, to everyone else I'm just plain Jane. I'd like to think I'm not too plain – I love books and stories after all.

I wasn't always a book designer. In fact I originally wanted to be an interior designer (as in home interiors, not book interiors). I went to college to study art and design, but it wasn't for me. I was too business-driven, too eager to get on and build a career, so I applied for a job in a graphic design firm making tea. Twelve months later and I was a full-time graphic designer, with my very own Apple Mac, working for clients including ASDA, Motorola, M&S, as well as lots of local businesses on branding and brochures, logos, leaflets, exhibitions, all kinds of corporate stuff.

Around 2001, my friend and colleague read some copy I'd written and said, 'It's really good. You should write.' And so I did.

I had two passions: design and writing, and in early 2012 they abruptly collided. I took voluntary redundancy and made the decision not to apply for another job – I couldn't imagine being at another agency, the soul-destroying work of creating adverts and receiving emails back from marketing people saying 'thanks, I'll pass it on to the newspaper'. I just couldn't face it.

I had worked on books before, but not full time, and now I was working almost exclusively on book design (as well as some advertising for Mitsubishi*). It was the best career move I have ever made. Now I work from home, engaging every day with hugely talented and enthusiastic people: authors.

It is the most rewarding job I have ever done. In sixteen years working as a graphic designer, I have never experienced such enthusiasm for the work I produce, nor such effective collaboration. Books are my passion and my hobby. It's why I love being immersed in the world of books so much.

Writers are incredibly lovely to work with. Enthusiastic about their work – they write because they want to, not because they have to – and it shows in the emails and enquiries and messages I receive every day. I sit at my desk encouraged and motivated by other authors, writers, booklovers …

I anticipated working from home as the loneliest occupation, but far from it. I have made many friends within the writing community, people who make working life a wonderful place to be, people like Triskele Books who persuaded me to publish my own work.

My reward, in addition to being able to support myself through my skills, are many emails of gratitude, wine, chocolates, cookies and flowers (*still waiting for the "thank you" car from Mitsubishi)! It should be the other way around. I should be thanking them for providing the means to do a job that I love.

You can find my **book design site** here:
www.jdsmith-design.co.uk

Facebook: www.facebook.com/jdsmithdesign/

Twitter: www.twitter.com/JDSmith_Design

I am also the author of several historical fiction novels, a member of the Triskele Books collective, editor of the writers' ezine Words with JAM, and the readers' review site Bookmuse.

Lightning Source UK Ltd.
Milton Keynes UK
UKHW020607080319
338726UK00009B/143/P

9 780957 616493